Receiving Jesus

My Guide to the Mass

Aimee and Colin MacIver

ASCENSION

West Chester, Pennsylvania

Nihil obstat: Msgr. J. Brian Bransfield, STD
                   Censor Librorum
                   October 25, 2022

Imprimatur: +Most Rev. Nelson J. Perez, DD
                   Archbishop of Philadelphia
                   November 3, 2022

Ascension
PO Box 1990
West Chester, PA 19380
1-800-376-0520
ascensionpress.com

Cover and interior design: Stella Ziegler, Sarah Stueve
Interior art: Mike Moyers, Stella Ziegler, Sarah Stueve. See additional illustration credits on page 100.

Printed in the United States of America

ISBN: 978-1-954881-78-5

Contents

RECEIVING JESUS
My Guide to the Mass

My name is

_____

The church I go to is called

_____

SIT

We sit down at Mass to listen well and talk to God.

STAND

We stand at Mass to be ready to act on the Word of God.

KNEEL

We kneel at Mass to show our reverence for Jesus in the Eucharist.

It's Time to Go to Mass!

WHAT ARE YOU GOING TO WEAR? WHO IS GOING WITH YOU? WHAT PARISH WILL YOU GO TO?

Of all the things you're going to do today, Mass is the most special because Jesus will be there. Because he loves you so much, he will be really and truly present in the Eucharist. The Eucharist will look like bread and wine, but it will really be Jesus. Mass is the only place this miracle happens. You will watch it happen! Jesus is glad to see you at Mass. He loves you, and he is happy you are coming to spend time with him.

Even before Mass begins, you can prepare to be with Jesus. Think about it now. At Mass, you will be close to Jesus and you can tell him anything.

- What do you want to tell him today?
- What do you want to thank him for?
- How do you need him to help you?

A good prayer before Mass is

"Jesus, help me listen to you today at Mass."

Another way we prepare our bodies for Mass is to **fast**. This means we don't eat or drink anything except water or medicine for one hour before receiving Communion. Feeling hungry for food helps us think about how our souls are hungry for Jesus.

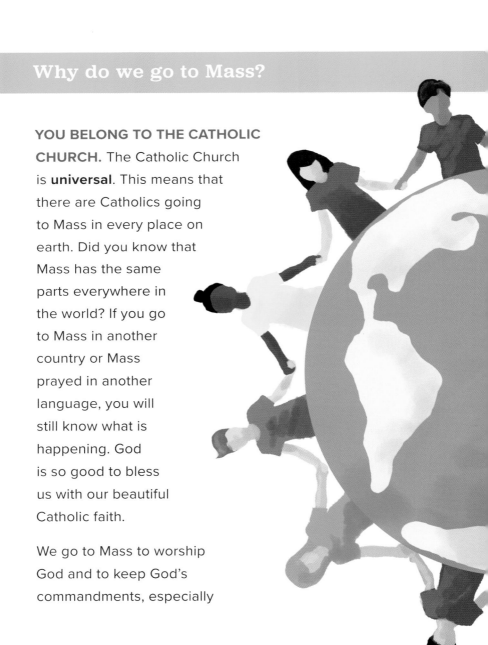

YOU BELONG TO THE CATHOLIC CHURCH. The Catholic Church is **universal**. This means that there are Catholics going to Mass in every place on earth. Did you know that Mass has the same parts everywhere in the world? If you go to Mass in another country or Mass prayed in another language, you will still know what is happening. God is so good to bless us with our beautiful Catholic faith.

We go to Mass to worship God and to keep God's commandments, especially

the commandment to keep the Sabbath day holy. God gave us the commandments to show us how to live a happy and holy life. To have a happy and holy life, it is important to spend time with Jesus. Every time you go to Mass, you spend time with Jesus. At Mass you worship God and show him that he is the most important person in your life. The more you love God first, the more you can love your family, your friends, and yourself. Going to Mass helps us grow stronger in love.

You are a human person with a soul and a body, so your worship of God is connected to things you can see, hear, touch, smell, and taste with your body.

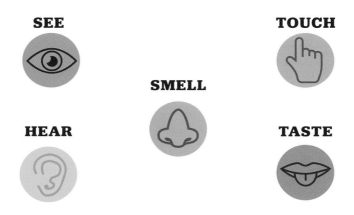

SEE

TOUCH

SMELL

HEAR

TASTE

When you go inside the church, do you see the holy water font? Holy water is a **sacramental**. Sacramentals are sacred signs that help us receive the full grace of the sacraments with a proper disposition. Holy water reminds us that we are God's children through our Baptism. Baptism was the very first sacrament that you received. Dip your fingers into the water and make the Sign of the Cross to let Jesus know you are here and ready to be with him.

This is how we make the Sign of the Cross

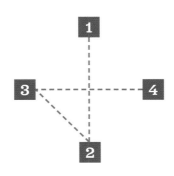

1

In the Name of the Father

With your right hand, touch your forehead.

2

and of the Son

Touch your chest.

3

and of the Holy

Touch your left shoulder.

4

Spirit.

Touch your right shoulder.

Amen.

WHICH PEW WILL YOU SIT IN? If you sit in the front, you will be able to see everything going on at Mass! You will be able to hear the music and the readings very well.

Look for the candles on the altar. How many do you see? We use candles for special occasions. The candles help us remember that Mass is the most special occasion of our lives.

Do you see the red candle near the **tabernacle**? This is the sanctuary light that tells us that Jesus in the Eucharist is inside the tabernacle right now!

Whenever you see the sanctuary light burning, **genuflect** toward the tabernacle to show Jesus that you know he is here and how much you love him.

What color cloth is on the altar today, and what color is the priest wearing? The different colors tell us what liturgical season or feast day is today.

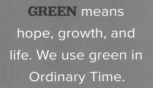

GREEN means hope, growth, and life. We use green in Ordinary Time.

RED means sacrifice. We use red for Palm Sunday, Good Friday, Pentecost, and the feasts of the Apostles and martyrs.

Being Catholic means being part of so many celebrations!

PINK (OR ROSE) means something good is coming! We use pink on the third Sunday of Advent and the fourth Sunday of Lent.

PURPLE means waiting or sorrow for sin. We use purple during Advent and Lent.

WHITE AND GOLD mean glory or purity. We use white or gold for Easter, for feasts of the Blessed Mother, and for saints who were not martyrs.

The Introductory Rites

Mass is beginning! Are you ready?

Stand up and join the song. We stand because the priest is leading us on a journey to the altar of God, and we are going with him. This is the processional. Sometimes it will just be the priest. But other times, there can be a number of different people! See who is there today!

Do you see altar servers carrying candles and a crucifix? The candles remind us that Jesus is the light of the world. The altar server holds the crucifix high to remind us of what Jesus said: "When I am lifted up, I will draw everyone to myself." Did you know that, after your first Reconciliation and first Communion, you can be an altar server too?

Who else do you see in the procession? Do you see any deacons or lectors (readers)? All these people will help the priest celebrate Mass—and so will you with your prayers and participation.

Do you see the priest? The priest is *in persona Christi*, which means he is representing Jesus in the prayer of the Mass.

Watch them bow toward the tabernacle when they reach the altar. Bowing shows that we know Jesus is here and that we love and respect him.

Do you think the altar looks like a table? It looks this way to remind us that Mass is like a special meal. Jesus in the Eucharist is food for our souls. The altar also reminds us that Mass is a **sacrifice**. A sacrifice is a holy gift given to God to show our love for him. At Mass, in the Eucharist, Jesus will give himself as a holy gift to God the Father and to us.

Many altars have special *relics* inside them. Relics are holy objects from a saint's body, like a piece of hair. Relics can also be from something a saint owned, like a little piece of his or her sweater. Ask your priest if the altar in your parish has any relics inside it. When the priest walks around to the back of the altar, he kisses it. Kissing the altar honors the relics and reminds us of the saints and angels who are with us at Mass.

Priest: In the name of the Father, and of the Son, and of the Holy Spirit.

YOU: Amen.

We begin Mass like other prayers with the Sign of the Cross. Mass is the greatest prayer of our faith. At Mass, you are praying the same prayer that all the saints prayed. At Mass, Mary and all the angels and saints in heaven join you in worshiping God. Which saints do you know? Ask your favorite saint to help you pray right now.

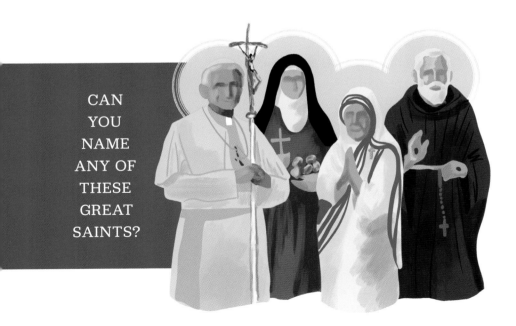

CAN YOU NAME ANY OF THESE GREAT SAINTS?

Greeting

The priest greets the **congregation**. The congregation is all the people at Mass with you. Every person at Mass is important, so it is important for every person to participate in the prayers and responses. We are not at Mass to watch the priest but to worship God together. You matter at Mass. You have important work to do with your mind, heart, voice, and body.

> **Priest:** The Lord be with you.
> **YOU:** *And with your spirit.*

These same words are sometimes used in the Bible when someone is being called to important work. "The Lord be with you" means you are being called by God!

Penitential Act

Now we will tell God we are sorry for our sins and ask him to forgive us. Sin hurts us and makes it harder for us to love God, others, and ourselves. But good news: God is happy when we ask for forgiveness. We should reconcile with God before we receive Jesus in the Eucharist, so we can be close to him with nothing in between!

We are reconciled with God when we go to Confession, so we should go to Confession often. However, the Penitential Act during Mass includes a general confession of sin that, when we pray, can forgive our venial sins. (But it is still good to confess those in the Sacrament of Reconciliation.)

This prayer is the *Confiteor*. You may hear it at some Masses. Pray it together with the priest and the congregation.

I confess to almighty God
and to you, my brothers and sisters,
that I have greatly sinned,
in my thoughts and in my words,
in what I have done and in what I have
failed to do,
through my fault, through my fault,
through my most grievous fault;
therefore I ask blessed Mary ever-Virgin,
all the Angels and Saints,
and you, my brothers and sisters,
to pray for me to the Lord our God.

This prayer is the **Kyrie**. Pray it together with the priest and the congregation. We have admitted to God our sins, and now we ask for his mercy.

> Priest: Lord, have mercy.
>
> **YOU: Lord, have mercy.**
>
> Priest: Christ, have mercy.
>
> **YOU: Christ, have mercy.**
>
> Priest: Lord, have mercy.
>
> **YOU: Lord, have mercy.**

Gloria

What should we do once God forgives our sins? We should praise and thank him! The **Gloria** is a song of praise from the Bible. The angels sang the first part of this prayer when Jesus was born in Bethlehem. You may say it or sing it.

Did you know that singing is a very special way to pray? St. Augustine said, "Those who sing pray twice." Sing boldly at Mass! God loves to hear your voice singing prayers to him. He thinks your voice sounds beautiful.

Glory to God in the highest,
and on earth peace to people of good will.
We praise you,
we bless you,
we adore you,
we glorify you,
we give you thanks for your great glory,
Lord God, heavenly King,
O God, almighty Father.
Lord Jesus Christ, Only Begotten Son,
Lord God, Lamb of God, Son of the Father,
you take away the sins of the world,
have mercy on us;
you take away the sins of the world,
receive our prayer;
you are seated at the right hand of the Father,
have mercy on us.
For you alone are the Holy One,
you alone are the Lord,
you alone are the Most High,
Jesus Christ,
with the Holy Spirit,
in the glory of God the Father.
Amen.

The Liturgy of the Word

The Readings and Responsorial Psalm

Now we sit down to hear readings from the Bible, God's Word. When we sit down it means that we are ready to listen to what God has to say to us. The Bible is an important way that God teaches us. The Bible is not a regular book but rather a book that the Holy Spirit wrote with human authors.

It tells the beginning of our story with God. Listen closely! Does anything in the first reading remind you of Jesus and his life? The Old Testament is filled with prophesies about Jesus a long time before he was born.

> **Reader:** The word of the Lord.
>
> *YOU: Thanks be to God.*

The *Responsorial Psalm* helps us think about what God teaches us in his Word. The Psalms are special songs for God. Many were written by King David, and we still sing them today. Say or sing the response together with the priest and the congregation.

The *Second Reading* is from the New Testament. The New Testament tells us about Jesus. God speaks to you in his Word. Make sure you listen closely! What is your favorite part of the second reading today?

Reader: The word of the Lord.
YOU: Thanks be to God.

Now sing the *Alleluia* and stand up for the Gospel. *Alleluia!* means "Praise God!"

Why do you think we stand, sit, kneel, and do other motions during Mass? These are ways we can use our bodies to worship God. Your body is good and holy because God made it.

In a moment, when you say "Glory to you, O Lord," use your thumb to trace a small cross on your forehead, your lips, and your heart. This is a way we ask the Holy Spirit to help us think about, talk about, and love Jesus.

Deacon (or Priest): The Lord be with you.

YOU: And with your spirit.

Deacon (or Priest): A reading from the holy Gospel according to N.

YOU: Glory to you, O Lord.

The Gospel tells us a story about Jesus' life. While you listen to the Gospel, can you imagine how Jesus looked? What do you think he was wearing? How do you think his voice sounded? The Gospel is an important way you can get to know Jesus. What is your favorite part of the Gospel today?

> **Deacon (or Priest):** The Gospel of the Lord.
> *YOU: Praise to you, Lord Jesus Christ.*

Homily

Sit down while the priest or deacon gives the homily. The homily helps us learn how to be holy from the readings. God made just one *you* in the whole world, so you are special! He made you to be holy and to be a saint. You grow in holiness by loving God, loving others, and avoiding sin.

Can you think of one way to grow in holiness this week?

Profession of Faith

Stand for the *Profession of Faith*. The Profession of Faith will be one of the ancient Creeds of the Church. Some parishes profess the Apostles' Creed. Many parishes profess the faith using the *Nicene Creed*. This is a very old prayer that Catholics have said since the fourth century. Can you imagine Catholics all over the world praying this prayer in different languages?

I believe in one God,
the Father almighty,
maker of heaven and earth,
of all things visible and invisible.
I believe in one Lord Jesus Christ,
the Only Begotten Son of God,
born of the Father before all ages.
God from God, Light from Light,
true God from true God,
begotten, not made, consubstantial with the Father;
through him all things were made.
For us men and for our salvation
he came down from heaven,
and by the Holy Spirit was incarnate of the
Virgin Mary,
and became man.

turn page

Ich glaube

私は信じている

For our sake he was crucified under Pontius Pilate,
he suffered death and was buried,
and rose again on the third day
in accordance with the Scriptures.
He ascended into heaven
and is seated at the right hand of the Father.
He will come again in glory
to judge the living and the dead
and his kingdom will have no end.
I believe in the Holy Spirit, the Lord, the giver of life,
who proceeds from the Father and the Son,
who with the Father and the Son is adored
and glorified,
who has spoken through the prophets.
I believe in one, holy, catholic and apostolic Church.
I confess one Baptism for the forgiveness of sins
and I look forward to the resurrection of the dead
and the life of the world to come. Amen.

Naamini

Universal Prayer
(Prayer of the Faithful)

The Church needs your help now to ask God for many important things. Your prayers matter because God hears them! Your prayers are powerful, so pray from your heart. Ask God to hear your prayer! God is so happy when we ask him for help, because this shows that we trust him.

Deacon or minister: We pray to the Lord.

YOU: Lord, hear our prayer.

God feeds our souls with his word to help us be holy. Now let's get ready for God to feed our bodies and souls with Jesus in the Eucharist!

The Liturgy of
the Eucharist

The Preparation of the Altar

We often have special meals to celebrate special occasions. How does your family set the table for special occasions? Watch the priest prepare the altar for the Eucharist. Sometimes deacons or altar servers help him. This is like setting the table for the most special occasion of all. Jesus will be here in the Eucharist very soon!

Can you find these special items?

The **MISSAL** is the book of prayers used during Mass.

The **CHALICE** holds the wine that becomes Jesus' blood.

The **PATON** holds the hosts that become Jesus' body.

Did you know that the chalice and ciborium are made of gold or silver? Gold and silver are very precious. We use precious metal to hold Jesus' Body and Blood because he is even more precious than gold, and we want to offer him the very best we have. The precious metals remind us that the Eucharist may look like bread and wine but is really Jesus coming to be close to you.

Do you see the small white cloths on the altar? After the consecration, Jesus is truly present in each drop of wine and crumb of the host, so we want to make sure none gets lost.

The **PURIFICATOR** is a cloth used to wipe any drops of wine from the chalice.

The **CORPORAL** is a cloth that goes under the chalice and the paton to catch any tiny drops of wine or crumbs of the host.

While the altar is prepared for Jesus, you can prepare your heart for Jesus.

A good prayer is

"Jesus, help me to be ready to receive you today."

You can ask Mary to help you receive Jesus just as she did. Mary held Jesus inside her body when she was pregnant with him. You will hold Jesus inside your body when you receive the Eucharist. Mary loves you and will always help you grow closer to God.

The Presentation of the Gifts

As the priest prepares the altar, the gift bearers will bring the bread and wine to him at the altar. Would you like to be a gift bearer someday?

The bread and wine are **offerings**. Offerings are gifts. What is a gift? You receive a gift from someone who loves you, and you give a gift to someone you love. We give these gifts to show our love for God and the Church.

God will make our simple gifts into the greatest gift of all—Jesus' real Body and Blood!

The Preparation of the Gifts

The priest blesses and prepares the bread and wine. Do you see him pour water into the wine? This reminds us that God the Son became man to save us. The priest will also pray these prayers out loud or quietly to himself. If he prays out loud, respond with the congregation.

Priest: Blessed are you, Lord God of all creation,
for through your goodness we have received
the bread we offer you:
fruit of the earth and work of human hands,
it will become for us the bread of life.
YOU: Blessed be God for ever.

Priest: Blessed are you, Lord God of all creation,
for through your goodness we have received
the wine we offer you: fruit of the vine and work of human hands,
it will become our spiritual drink.
YOU: Blessed be God for ever.

Now the ushers may pass a basket to take the collection. Jesus commanded the Church to help the poor and do other good work in the world. The Church is all of us! You are the Church. We share our own money to help the Church's work. God loves when we share. Do you remember the boy who gave Jesus five loaves and two fish? Jesus multiplied the boy's gift to help a whole crowd.

Our collection at Mass is like this. Everything we give to God, he makes into something greater. You are also a gift to your family and the world. Offer yourself as a gift back to God. He will make you into something even greater!

What can you offer to Jesus as a gift?

- **Your time**: Give Jesus your participation in Mass and a few minutes of prayer every day.

- **Your talent**: Use your talents to serve others and glorify God.

- **Your treasure**: Share money and things you have with others.

Do you see the priest wash his hands? This reminds us of our Baptism and that we need to be cleansed of our sins.

Priest: Pray, brethren, that my sacrifice and yours may be acceptable to God, the almighty Father.

YOU: May the Lord accept the sacrifice at your hands for the praise and glory of his name, for our good and the good of all his holy Church.

Eucharistic Prayer

The Eucharistic Prayer is the most important part of Mass. Are you excited? A great miracle will happen soon. You will see it with your own eyes of faith! The bread and wine will become Jesus' real Body and Blood.

Remember that you are not just watching the priest. You are a very important part of the prayer. Think about the words you are saying. God gives us so many blessings. What he wants from us is our hearts. Lift up your heart to God when you pray.

Priest: The Lord be with you.

YOU: And with your spirit.

Priest: Lift up your hearts.

YOU: We lift them up to the Lord.

Priest: Let us give thanks to the Lord our God.

YOU: It is right and just.

The Eucharistic Prayer is about the great sacrifice Jesus made when he died to save us. How much must Jesus love you to die so you could go to heaven? Now we sing a prayer of praise for God's goodness. Sing the prayer from your heart with the priest and the congregation.

Holy, Holy, Holy Lord God of hosts.

Heaven and earth are full of your glory.

Hosanna in the highest.

Blessed is he who comes in the name of the Lord.

Hosanna in the highest.

Now we kneel down. Kneeling is a way your body can show honor and respect to God. Kneeling also shows that you know God's power, that you trust God's goodness, and that you want to do what God wants.

Jesus himself began the Eucharistic prayer at the Last Supper. Listen to the priest say the exact same words that Jesus said to his friends. You are Jesus' friend, too. This means that when you are at Mass, you are joining Jesus at the Last Supper and Jesus on the Cross. It is not magic but a miracle.

The priest asks the Holy Spirit to come upon the gifts. This is called the **epiclesis**. Then, at the prayer of **consecration**, the bread and wine become Jesus! This change is called **transubstantiation**.

> The bread and wine will still look, taste, and feel like bread and wine, but they will really be Jesus' Body and Blood.

During these prayers, the altar servers may ring bells to help us focus on the miracle that is happening.

At the consecration, the priest is not offering a new sacrifice to God. He is offering the *exact same* sacrifice that Jesus offered to God the Father when he died on the Cross—his own Body and Blood. Remember that Jesus also rose from the dead! When you receive Jesus in the Eucharist, you receive the whole risen and living Jesus.

Priest: Take this, all of you, and eat of it,
for this is my Body,
which will be given up for you.

Watch the priest lift up Jesus' Body now just as Jesus' Body was lifted up on the Cross. Bow your head to show Jesus you know he is here and you love him so much.

Priest: Take this, all of you, and drink from it,
for this is the chalice of my Blood,
the Blood of the new and eternal covenant,
which will be poured out for you and for many
for the forgiveness of sins.
Do this in memory of me.

Watch the priest lift up Jesus' Blood in the chalice. Bow your head to show Jesus you know he is here and you love him so much.

This prayer is the *mystery of faith*. Only one of these will be chosen during the Mass. Pray it together with the priest and the congregation.

We proclaim your Death, O Lord,
and profess your Resurrection,
until you come again.

OR

When we eat this Bread and drink this Cup,
we proclaim your Death, O Lord,
until you come again.

OR

Save us, Savior of the world,
for by your Cross and Resurrection,
you have set us free.

At the end of the Eucharistic Prayer, the priest raises the chalice and the host and says,

> **Priest:** Through him, and with him, and in him,
> O God, almighty Father,
> in the unity of the Holy Spirit,
> all glory and honor is yours,
> for ever and ever.

Like all prayers, the Eucharistic Prayer ends with **Amen.** This Amen is called "The Great Amen." Mass is the greatest prayer because Jesus is really here.

All: Amen.

The Communion Rite

The Lord's Prayer

Jesus told us how to pray to God the Father. God is happy when we pray because it shows we trust him. We praise God for being so good. We ask God to give us what we need. God will always do what is best for us. We also ask God to forgive us and help us avoid sin. We try to reconcile with God before we receive Jesus in the Eucharist. Stand to pray with the priest and the congregation.

ALL:

Our Father, who art in heaven,

hallowed be thy name;

thy kingdom come,

thy will be done

on earth as it is in heaven.

Give us this day our daily bread,

and forgive us our trespasses,

as we forgive those who trespass against us;

and lead us not into temptation,

but deliver us from evil.

PRIEST:

Deliver us, Lord, we pray, from every evil,

graciously grant us peace in our days,

that, by the help of your mercy,

we may be always free from sin

and safe from all distress,

as we await the blessed hope

and the coming of our Savior, Jesus Christ.

YOU:

For the kingdom,

the power and the glory are yours

now and for ever.

Sign of Peace

The sign of peace reminds us that God's people are a family. We should love each other as we love our own families. This is also a way we reconcile with others before we receive Jesus in the Eucharist.

Priest: The peace of the Lord be with you always.

YOU: And with your spirit.

Priest: Let us offer each other the sign of peace.

Give the people near you a sign of peace (for example, a handshake, a wave, or a smile).

Lamb of God

This prayer reminds us that Jesus took away our sins so we could go to heaven. Jesus is the Lamb of God.

> *Lamb of God, you take away the sins of the world,*
> *have mercy on us.*
> *Lamb of God, you take away the sins of the world,*
> *have mercy on us.*
> *Lamb of God, you take away the sins of the world,*
> *grant us peace.*

Fraction Rite

Watch the priest carefully. Do you see him break the consecrated host and put a piece into the chalice? The host is Jesus' body. Breaking the host reminds us that Jesus' body was broken to save us. Kneel down to show Jesus you are thankful for his sacrifice.

> **Priest:** Behold the Lamb of God,
> behold him who takes away the sins of the world.
> Blessed are those called to the supper of the Lamb.
>
> *YOU: Lord, I am not worthy*
> *that you should enter under my roof,*
> *but only say the word*
> *and my soul shall be healed.*

Communion

The most amazing thing you will ever do is about to happen! You are going to receive Jesus himself in the Eucharist. He became man, suffered, died, and rose again just to save you and bring you to heaven. You are so precious to him. He wants to hear everything that you want to tell him.

Go up to the altar reverently. Your body helps you to worship. Fold your hands into prayer hands. Look at Jesus and think about Jesus. Make your heart quiet so you can hear what he says. The congregation walking toward the altar to receive Jesus reminds us that we journey toward heaven together.

Receiving Holy Communion is very serious because it is really Jesus. We must not receive Jesus if we have mortal sins that we still need to confess in the Sacrament of Reconciliation. If you are not ready to receive Holy Communion today, cross your arms across your heart for a blessing.

Bow down before your turn to receive Holy Communion. The minister will lift up Jesus in the Host, just as he was lifted up on the Cross to save you. When you say "Amen," this means you believe Jesus is really here and that you are ready to receive him.

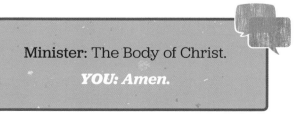

Minister: The Body of Christ.

YOU: Amen.

DID YOU KNOW?

There are two ways you may receive the Host: on your tongue or in your hands.

On your tongue: Open your mouth and put out your tongue past your teeth and lips. The minister will place the Host on your tongue. Step to the side and consume the Host reverently as you go back to your pew.

In your hands: Make sure your hands are clean. Put your writing hand under your other hand. This makes a small throne for Jesus. The minister will place the Host into your hands. Step to the side, put the Host in your mouth, and consume it reverently as you go back to your pew.

The consecrated wine in the chalice is also really Jesus. You can receive Jesus from the chalice like this:

Bow down before your turn to receive the chalice. The minister will lift up Jesus in the chalice just as he was lifted up on the Cross to save you. When you say "Amen," this means you believe Jesus is really here and that you are ready to receive him.

Minister: The Blood of Christ.

YOU: Amen.

Place both hands around the top of the chalice and take a small sip. Then carefully give the chalice back to the minister.

Prayer After Communion

When you get back to your pew, this is your most special time with Jesus. Your body has become a tabernacle! Kneel down to talk to Jesus from your heart. Ask him for what you need. Tell him how you need his help. Most of all, worship him.

A good prayer to worship Jesus is

**"I love you, Jesus. You are my God.
Help me to love you more."**

The Concluding Rites

The word *Mass* means *sent.* At the end of Mass, you are sent by God to share the good news with the rest of the world. You have just been with Jesus at the Last Supper and on the Cross! You have just been with Mary and all the angels and all the saints! Jesus in the Eucharist is now part of your body. Being so close to Jesus will help bring God's love to others. Are you ready?

Solemn Blessing

Priest: *The Lord be with you.*
YOU: *And with your spirit.*

Final Blessing

The priest will bless you on your way out of Mass! This is so that you are strengthened and prepared to go out and love and serve others.

Priest: *May almighty God bless you,*
the Father, and the Son, and the Holy Spirit.
YOU: *Amen.*

Dismissal

Deacon (or Priest): *Go forth, the Mass is ended.*
YOU: *Thanks be to God.*

Jesus is happy
you came to
Mass today.

Catholic Prayers

Sign of the Cross

In the name of the Father,
and of the Son,
and of the Holy Spirit.
Amen.

Our Father

Our Father, who art in heaven,
hallowed be thy name;
thy kingdom come,
thy will be done
on earth as it is in heaven.
Give us this day our daily bread,
and forgive us our trespasses,
as we forgive those who trespass against us;
and lead us not into temptation,
but deliver us from evil.
Amen.

Apostles' Creed

I believe in God,
the Father almighty,
Creator of heaven and earth,
and in Jesus Christ, his only Son, our Lord,
who was conceived by the Holy Spirit,
born of the Virgin Mary,
suffered under Pontius Pilate,
was crucified, died and was buried;
he descended into hell;
on the third day he rose again from the dead;
he ascended into heaven,
and is seated at the right hand
of God the Father almighty;
from there he will come to judge
the living and the dead.
I believe in the Holy Spirit,
the holy catholic Church,
the communion of saints,
the forgiveness of sins,
the resurrection of the body,
and life everlasting. Amen.

Hail Mary

Hail, Mary, full of grace,
the Lord is with thee.
Blessed art thou among women,
and blessed is the
fruit of thy womb, Jesus.
Holy Mary, Mother of God,
pray for us sinners
now and at the hour of our death.
Amen.

Glory Be

Glory be to the Father and to the
Son and to the Holy Spirit,
as it was in the beginning,
is now, and ever shall be,
world without end,
Amen.

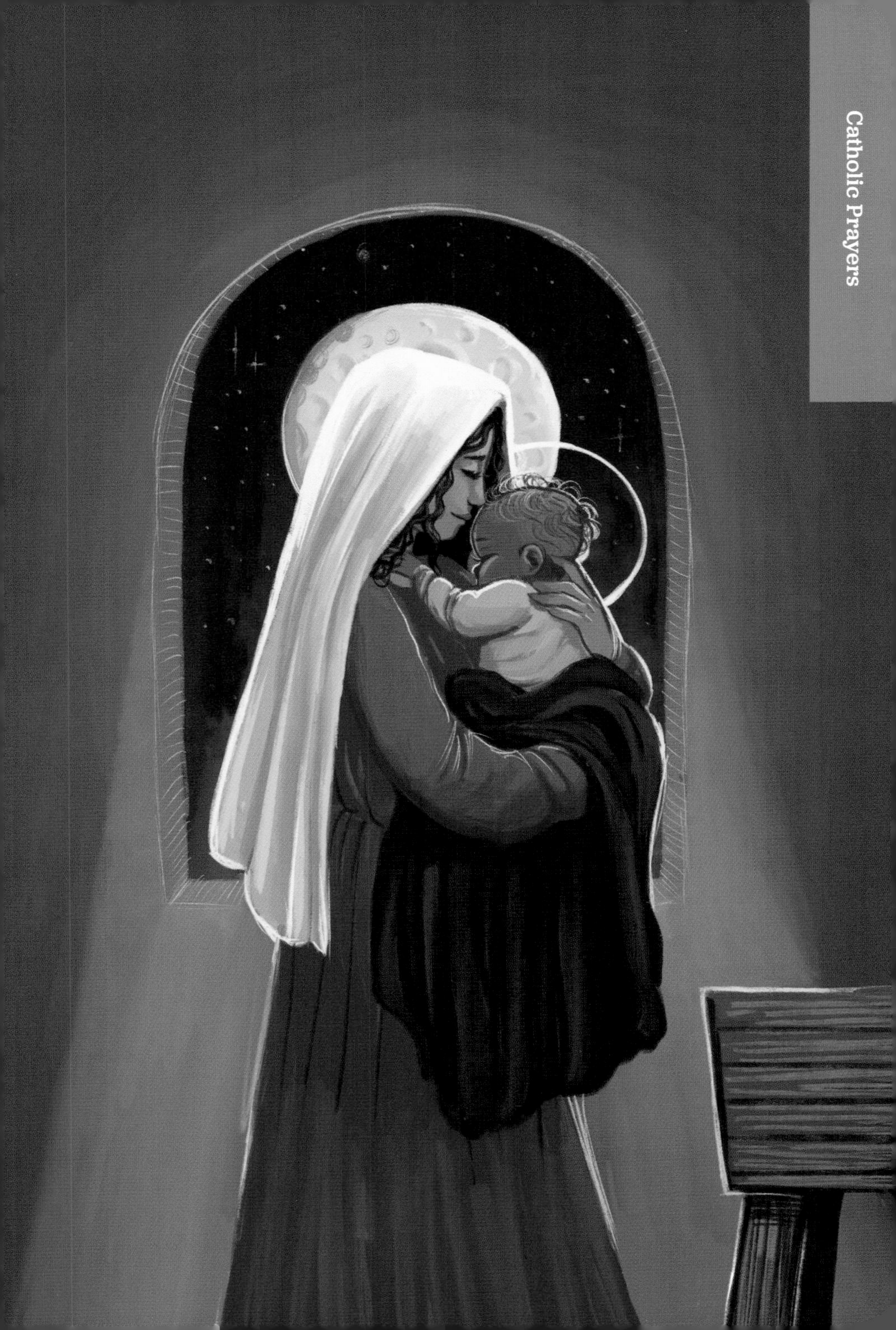

Memorare

Remember, O most gracious Virgin Mary,
that never was it known that anyone
who fled to thy protection,
implored thy help, or sought thine
intercession was left unaided.
Inspired by this confidence, I fly unto
thee, O Virgin of virgins, my mother;
to thee do I come, before thee I
stand, sinful and sorrowful.
O Mother of the Word Incarnate,
despise not my petitions,
but in thy mercy hear and answer me.
Amen.

Fatima Prayer

O my Jesus, forgive us our sins.
Save us from the fires of hell.
Lead all souls to heaven, especially those
in most need of thy mercy. Amen.

Grace Before Meals

Bless us, O Lord, and these thy gifts,
which we are about to receive
from thy bounty,
through Christ our Lord.
Amen.

Thanksgiving After Meals

We give thanks for all your
benefits, almighty God,
who lives and reigns forever.
May the souls of the faithful departed,
through the mercy of God, rest in peace.
Amen.

St. Michael the Archangel

St. Michael the Archangel, defend us in battle.
Be our protection against the
wickedness and snares of the devil.
May God rebuke him, we
humbly pray. And do thou,
O Prince of the heavenly host,
by the power of God,
cast into hell Satan and all the evil spirits
who prowl through the world
seeking the ruin of souls.
Amen.

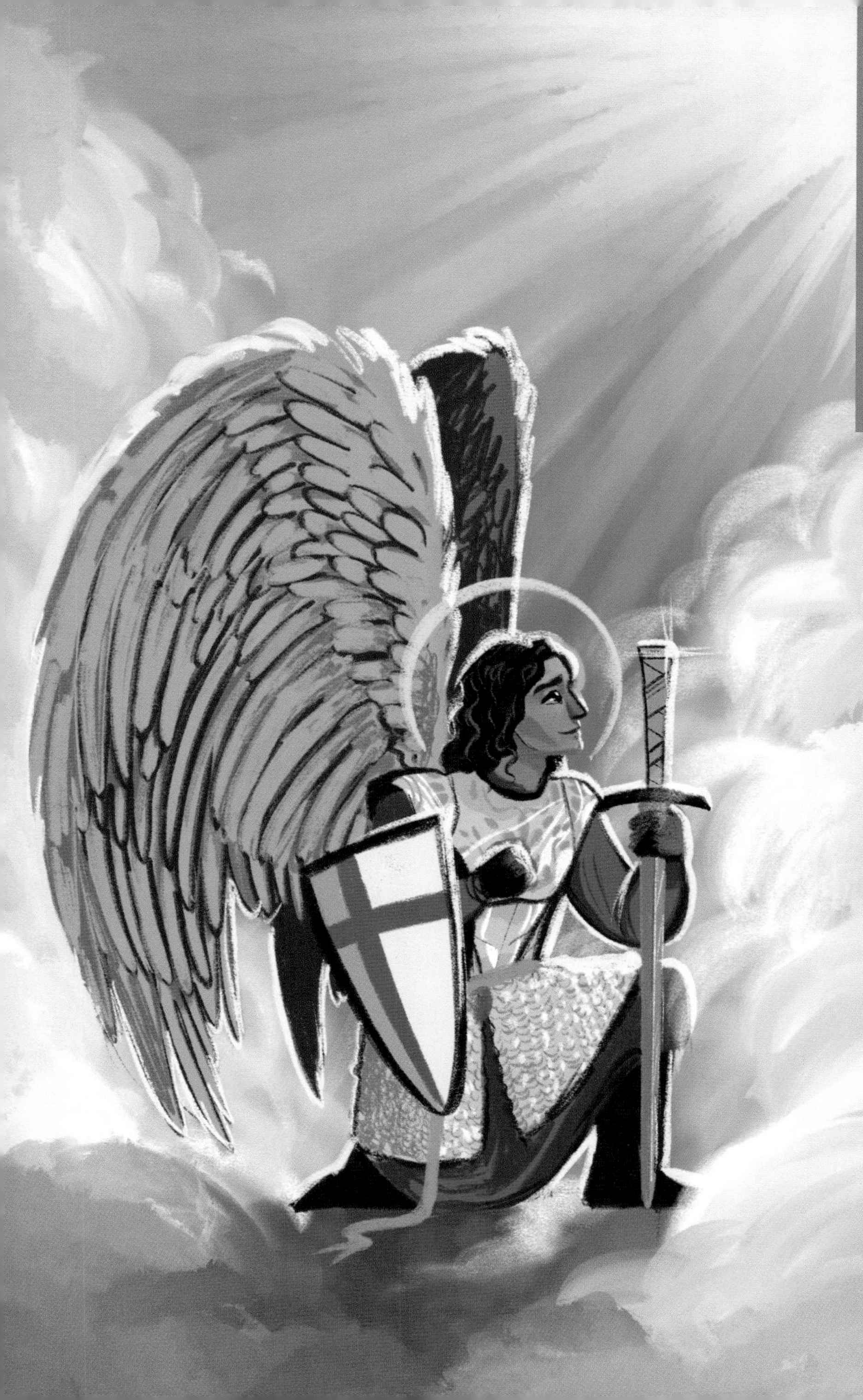

Prayer to my Guardian Angel

Angel of God, my guardian dear,
to whom God's love commits me here,
ever this day, be at my side,
to light and guard, to rule and guide.
Amen.

An Act of Spiritual Communion

My Jesus,
I believe that You
are present in the Most Holy Sacrament.
I love you above all things,
and I desire to receive you into my soul.
Since I cannot at this moment
receive you sacramentally,
come at least spiritually into my heart.
I embrace you as if you were already there
and unite myself wholly to you.
Never permit me to be separated from you.
Amen.

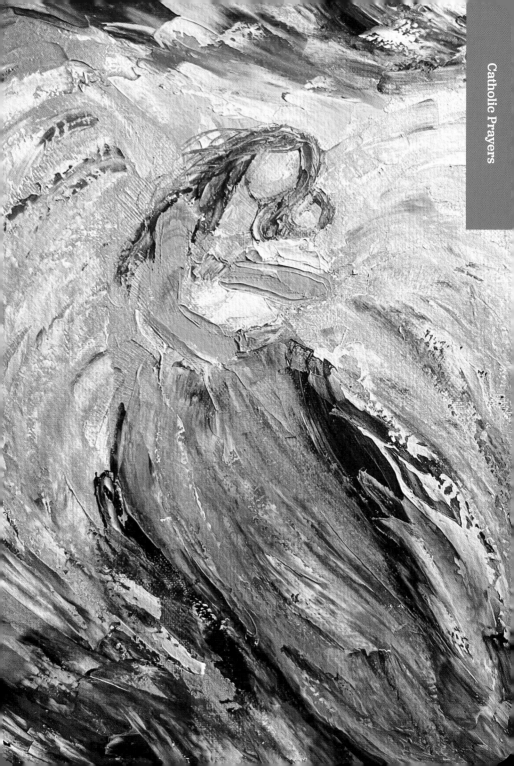

Knowing Your Catholic Faith

Saints

Here is a little secret. Okay, it's not really a secret. You are called to be a saint! Don't worry, it doesn't mean you have to wear a robe or that you are going to get turned into a statue.

The word "saint" refers to everybody in heaven. And you were made to go to heaven!

Who is your favorite saint? Do you know what it takes to be a saint? Follow the steps below and you'll become one:

- Follow the teachings of Christ and his Church.
- Go to Reconciliation when you commit a sin.
- Receive Jesus in the Holy Eucharist as often as you can.
- Live your life for Jesus!

Vocations in the Church

Christ is the source of ministry in the Church. He founded the Church. The power that the Church has is from Jesus. When he gathered together his disciples, he gave them the power to serve the Church as priests. He made Peter the first pope! Why did Jesus make the Church? So that the People of God could go to heaven.

The Mass itself came from Jesus and was given to us through his Apostles. Did you know that we still have apostolic succession today, with our bishops?

The priest in your parish was ordained by a bishop who can trace his ministry all the way back to the original Twelve Apostles chosen by Jesus. Here is some information about the Church as it is now.

Pope

Every pope has the job of St. Peter. Jesus gave Peter the keys to the kingdom of heaven when he said,

"And I tell you, you are Peter, and on this rock I will build my Church, and the gates of Hades shall not prevail against it. I will give you the keys of the kingdom of heaven, and whatever you bind on earth shall be bound in heaven, and whatever you loose on earth shall be loosed in heaven."

Matthew 16:18–19

The pope is not only the Bishop of Rome but also the Holy Father of the whole universal Catholic Church. He is the earthly representative of Christ and the pastor (shepherd) of the entire Church. He has full, supreme, and universal power over the whole Church throughout the world.

The pope has been given authority given by Jesus himself and is even guaranteed to teach the truth in matters of faith and morals.

Cardinal

A cardinal is a high-ranking person, almost always a bishop, who has been appointed by the pope to a special group called the College of Cardinals. The main duty of a cardinal is to help when a new pope needs to be elected. Cardinals also serve on the governing body of the Church.

Archbishop/Bishop

Bishops have received the fullness of the Sacrament of Holy Orders, which makes them successors of the Apostles. A bishop is the shepherd of a particular church or diocese entrusted to him. An archbishop is the bishop of an archdiocese; an archdiocese has a larger population of Catholics and is therefore often "bigger" than a diocese. Bishops are the visible source and foundation of unity in their own churches and are assisted by priests and deacons.

Priest

Priests are members of the order of priesthood, the second degree of the Sacrament of Holy Orders. They are coworkers with their bishops and are dedicated to helping their bishops in priestly service to the People of God. Through the ministry of priests, the unique sacrifice of Christ on the Cross is made present in the Eucharistic sacrifice of the Church.

Deacon

The diaconate is the third degree of the hierarchy of the Sacrament of Holy Orders, after bishop and priest. The deacon is ordained not to priesthood but for ministry and service. Deacons are ordained to assist the bishop and priests in celebrating the divine mysteries, especially the Eucharist, in distributing Holy Communion. They also assist at and bless marriages, proclaim the Gospel and preach, preside at funerals, and dedicate themselves to the various ministries of charity.

Religious and Consecrated

Some are called to a special relationship with God in a religious vocation. They may be part of an order that lives out a special service to the Church in prayer, teaching, healing, preaching, or even media. They may be men or women. Some are also priests, while others are brothers or sisters. People in religious life and consecrated life make special promises or vows. Some of these include vows of poverty (not owning their own property), chastity (not being married to anyone but Christ and the Church), and obedience (listening to a superior).

Laity

The laity are the faithful, who by Baptism are part of the body of Christ and members of the People of God. Everyone who is baptized shares in the priestly, prophetic, and kingly office of Christ and has their own part to play in the mission of the whole Church and in the world.

Who's Who in the Liturgy

Who's Who

Now that we've taken a look at the different roles, ministries, and vocations in the bigger picture of the Church, let's look at some of the different ministries that we see in the Mass itself. Mass is not a show that we watch, and it is important to understand that everyone has a full, conscious, and active

in the Liturgy

role in what's happening. There are some specific roles, though, and we will take a look at who and what you might see in your own parish. Some of these ministries are things that you could be involved in very soon in your own parish, while others might be roles and ministries that you are called to later on in life.

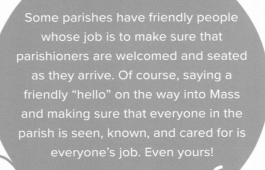

Some parishes have friendly people whose job is to make sure that parishioners are welcomed and seated as they arrive. Of course, saying a friendly "hello" on the way into Mass and making sure that everyone in the parish is seen, known, and cared for is everyone's job. Even yours!

GREETERS

You will probably see that during the offertory there are some members of the congregation who bring up the bread and wine that will later become the body and blood of Christ during the Eucharistic Prayer.

GIFT BEARERS

The cantor leads everyone in song. It is especially important to lead the congregation in singing the Responsorial Psalm, *Alleluia*, and other Mass parts.

CANTOR

There may be a whole group of singers whose job is to pray in song and lead the congregation deeper into worship. The choir or schola is not there to put on a concert, but to express the beauty of the Mass in a way that helps others to pray well.

CHOIR (SCHOLA)

Ushers assist with the collection that takes place during the offertory. In the collection, families make an offering to God by supporting the work of their parish so that the parish can take care of keeping up the church, providing ministry, and supporting the poor in the parish.

USHERS

Lectors read the Word of God at Mass. This is a very important job! A lector will read the First and Second Readings, sometimes the Psalm, and sometimes the Prayer of the Faithful too. They have been chosen from the parish for a special ministry.

LECTORS

The pastor of the parish will often commission people to be extraordinary ministers of Holy Communion to help distribute the Eucharist during Mass and to the sick who are not able to attend Mass in person.

EXTRAORDINARY MINISTERS

97

The priest, who could even be a bishop depending on the Mass, is called the celebrant. The priest stands in the person of Jesus. who offers himself to God the Father in perfect love.

PRIEST OR BISHOP

Deacons have an important role in the Mass too! You might not see a deacon at every Mass, but they are often there to proclaim the Gospel, assist the priest at the altar, and sometimes to even preach the homily. Their role goes all the way back to St. Stephen, the first deacon mentioned in the Acts of the Apostles.

DEACONS

The altar servers' job is to help the priest with the celebration of the Mass. They help with everything from holding the Missal (a big important book with all the prayers for the Mass inside of it) for the priest to assisting with the gifts at the offertory.

ALTAR SERVERS

Illustration Credits

The following works are reprinted by permission from the Student Workbooks for *Renewed: Your Journey to Reconciliation* and *Received: Your Journey to Holy Communion* © 2023 Ascension Publishing Group, LLC:

69   *Their Angels in Heaven* by Jacob Flores-Popčak

71   *Reality of the Mass* by Chris Lewis, Baritus Catholic Illustration

73   *Mary, the Mother of God* by Liz Blair

75   *Children of Fatima* by Liz Blair

77   *Fresco of the Last Supper of Christ* by Leopold Kupelwieser

79   *St. Michael the Archangel* by Liz Blair

81   *Guardian Angel* by Karen Tarlton

Meet the Authors

Aimee and Colin MacIver are a husband-and-wife team who have been teaching, writing, and ministering together for more than twenty years. They are also parents who have learned many powerful lessons from their children.

When their son completed his first Reconciliation, he said, "My heart is free! Thank you, Jesus, for forgiving my sins!" When their daughter prepared for her first Communion, she asked, "Is Jesus wearing a bread costume?" Children have a true gift for teaching adults about God's wonder and beauty.

Colin and Aimee have coauthored several resources about the sacraments, including *Belonging: Baptism in the Family of God*; *Chosen: Your Journey Toward Confirmation*; *Connected: Catholic Social Teaching for This Generation*; and *Power and Grace: Your Guide to the Catholic Sacraments*.